ADVENTURES IN COLONIAL AMERICA

BLUE FEATHER'S VISION

The Dawn of Colonial America

by James E. Knight

illustrated by George Guzzi

Cover art by Shi Chen.

Library of Congress Cataloging-in-Publication Data

Knight, James E.
   Blue Feather's vision.

   Summary: An aged Indian chief fears that
white strangers who have visited his village
will return to destroy the Indian way of life.
   1. Massachuset Indians—First contact with
Occidental civilization—Juvenile literature.
2. Indians of North America—Massachusetts—
First contact with Occidental civilization—
Juvenile literature.   3. Massachusetts—His-
tory—Colonial period, ca. 1600–1775—Juvenile literature.   [1. Massachuset Indians.
2. Indians of North America—Massachusetts.
3. America—Discovery and exploration—English.]
I. Guzzi, George, ill.   II. title.
E99.M42K54   974.4'00497   81-23082
ISBN 0-89375-722-5   AACR2
ISBN 0-8167-4553-6 (pbk.)

This edition published 1998 by Troll Communications L.L.C.

Printed in the United States of America.

10   9   8   7   6   5

ADVENTURES IN COLONIAL AMERICA

BLUE FEATHER'S VISION

The Dawn of Colonial America

The old man sat nodding in the summer sun. His name was Blue Feather. Once he had been a great chief and warrior of the Massachuset tribe. Now he fought no longer, and his step was slow. Others had taken their places as chiefs and warriors among his people. Blue Feather had lived many long years.

Blue Feather nodded, but he was not asleep. He could hear the laughter of Bright Star as she sat on the beach making moccasins. Bright Star was twelve years old. She was the only child of Wamasoit, Blue Feather's oldest son. Wamasoit had been felled by a Pequot arrow in battle. Now Bright Star lived in Blue Feather's wigwam and cared for her grandfather. She was the joy of Blue Feather's life.

Bright Star dropped her work and came to Blue Feather's side. "Are you hungry, Grandfather?" she said.

Blue Feather opened his eyes and shook his head. "Do not worry over me, my child," he said softly. "I need nothing. I am content."

But Blue Feather was not content. Bright Star knew that her grandfather was troubled. Yet he would not speak of his fears to her, and she dared not mention them.

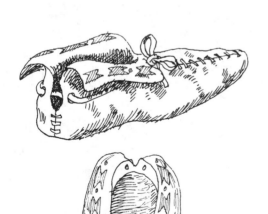

With a sad heart, Bright Star returned to her work. Nearby, two young braves were sealing the seams of a bark canoe with spruce gum. Bright Star watched them for a moment. Then she picked up the moccasin she was making.

Bright Star was very proud of her skill at making moccasins. First, she sewed a single piece of deerskin up the back and front. She left a cuff at the ankle to be tied with leather thongs. Then she sewed porcupine quills to the deerskin. When the moccasins were done, Bright Star would trade them for deer meat or a few fish.

Bright Star sighed. "Grandfather sits outside his wigwam in the warm sun," she thought. "He watches the

6

bluebird and finds comfort in its song. But his thoughts are not on the bluebird. I do not know what his thoughts are, but I believe he sees great trouble for our people. For that could be the only thing that would bother him so."

Bright Star was right. Her grandfather *was* deeply troubled. But a wise old chief of the Massachuset could not speak of his worries to a child. Instead, he talked to the Great Spirit, called Manitou. Manitou ruled the Algonkin nation, to which the Massachuset people belonged.

"You do not answer me, Great Spirit, but I know you hear," said Blue Feather. "You bring comfort to my old age.

"Nearly seventy snows have melted in this land of our fathers by the Great Sea. My life has been long and fruitful. My first son, Wamasoit, was killed in battle with the Pequot. But my other children live, though they make their homes in other villages. I have stood in battle with our brothers, the Narragansett and the Wampanoag. I have earned the pride of a warrior with my arrows. I have smoked the pipe of peace with great chiefs. I have known joy, and I have known sorrow. But what troubles me now, in the years of my late age, will not go away.

7

"My worries are not for myself, Great Spirit. For my time is near at hand. My worries are for my people, for my sons and my daughters, and for my granddaughter, Bright Star. It is as though I have a vision, Great Spirit of the Algonkin. And the vision tells me that my people will be destroyed. Not by the arrow of a warrior, like the Pequot. They will be destroyed by the strange men who come in the Great White Canoe of Many Wings."

Blue Feather's thoughts drifted back to nearly nine months past. And this is what he remembered:

A Great White Canoe sailed into the bay of the Massachuset. Its sails were like great wings, too many to count.

Blue Feather had seen white men before, when he was younger. But he had never seen so many as this time.

8

Friend

Eat

Thank You

Blue Feather's people watched in fear and awe as the Great White Canoe sailed toward them. They said not a word until the Great Canoe was quiet in the water. Then they began to whisper among themselves. For the pale-faced men launched small canoes and came ashore. They were strange to look upon, with their white skin. The leaders were dressed in shining white metal. And many of them carried thundersticks.

Blue Feather's people greeted these strangers in friendship. They gave the white men deer meat and corn. Then the white leader stepped forward and spoke.

"We are called English," he said. "And we have sailed from our home, called England, far across the Great Sea." The leader and Blue Feather could not understand each other's language. But they made their thoughts known with hand language.

Blue Feather invited the leader into his wigwam to smoke the pipe of peace. The white leader told him that before many more winters would come to pass, many English would come to these shores. Blue Feather's heart grew heavy.

For three days, the strangers stayed with Blue Feather and his people. The red men and the white men learned many things about each other. But there were still many things they did not understand.

One day the white chief drew marks in the sand and showed them to Blue Feather. The marks were "1591." Blue Feather shook his head. He did not understand. But he did not forget the marks.

———————

"I see you sleep in the sun, Father," said a laughing voice.

Blue Feather looked up, startled. Then he put out his hand to his youngest son. "I am glad to see you, Little Bear," he said. "It has been many sunsets since you have visited our village."

Little Bear sat upon the ground next to his father. "There is much work to be done," he said. "I have just finished my new wigwam. I have built it well, as you taught me."

"Tell me of your skills," said Blue Feather, "for it pleases me to hear of them."

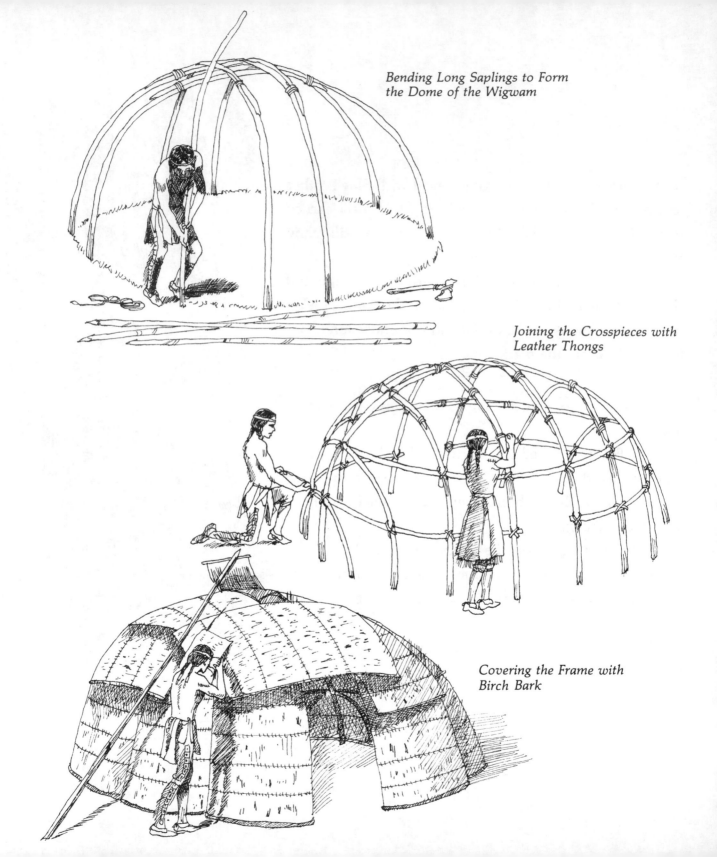

Bending Long Saplings to Form
the Dome of the Wigwam

Joining the Crosspieces with
Leather Thongs

Covering the Frame with
Birch Bark

Little Bear nodded. "First, I formed the dome of the house," he said. "I bent long saplings into semicircles and set them in the ground. Then I cut and joined crosspieces. Windsong, my squaw, helped me to tie the pieces together with leather thongs. Our young son is still too small to help." Little Bear smiled. "He sits in his bark crib and claps his hands. Then he laughs to see us so hard at work."

"What did you use to cover your new wigwam?" Blue Feather asked.

"I covered the frame with birch bark," said Little Bear. "I could have used deerskin or cornhusks or the mats that Windsong weaves from rushes. But I was lucky. I found enough birch bark to cover all of the wigwam. And I left a hole at the top of the wigwam for the smoke to escape through when Windsong tends her cooking."

Blue Feather was pleased. "You have done well," he said. "A brave must always see that his family has good shelter."

"And you are well, my father?" asked Little Bear.

"I am old," said Blue Feather in reply. "And my thoughts dwell on the white men, who will come again."

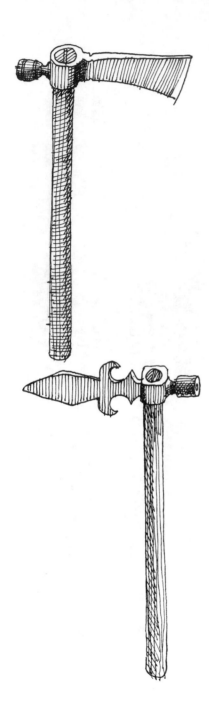

Little Bear shook his head. "Those are indeed an old man's thoughts, my father," he said. "The white men will not trouble us. They are no match for the strength of our warriors."

Blue Feather heard the words of his son. But he knew that Little Bear was wrong. He silently thought back to the day the English had left, so many moons ago.

The sun was climbing high as the white men prepared to sail away. The wings of the Great White Canoe were already set. Then the trouble began. One of the English chiefs said that shiny axes had been stolen. He said that young braves had stolen them. Blue Feather questioned the young men of the village. But there were no axes among them.

Then a young brave stepped forward. He said that a visiting Wampanoag named Wassaja took the axes. But Wassaja had already left the village. He was going to trade the axes among his own people.

The white chief grew angry and shook his fist. Then the warriors of the English captured two young braves.

16

Blue Feather watched in horror as the English pointed their dreaded weapons at the young men. Suddenly, great thunder spread across the water. The young braves lay dead on the beach. And the Great White Canoe quickly sailed out of the bay.

"Little Bear is wrong," thought Blue Feather. "There is bad blood between us and the palefaces. We are enemies. The white men are not gods, as some of our people think. They are only people, like us. But they are clever people. They have learned to make frightening things, like thundersticks and great canoes. We do not have this knowledge. And so they are stronger.

"We live with nature and the spirits. We live in harmony with our land. But these strange people have conquered their surroundings. Perhaps they have conquered nature. They will return, and they will conquer us. That is my vision. And that is the great fear that rests upon my mind."

Little Bear saw the unhappy look on his father's face. "You worry too much, Father," he said. "I know that the visits of these white men have confused some of our young braves. They see knives and axes made of metal. And they want them. They would trade many long belts of wampum for them. They even question our old ways, the ways you have taught me. Some say that when the white men return, these braves will go to live with them and learn their ways. But I do not believe this will happen."

Blue Feather nodded. "Yes, my son, it will come to pass. This I know. For more than seventy winters, I have hunted these forests and fished these waters. I have loved this land, and it has been good to me. But hear my vision.

"The time is soon at hand when the red man of the forest will leave the land of his birth. Far beyond the long houses of the Iroquois, he will look for new land. For these white men who come in their Great Canoes will take this land we cherish, these beaches we love. We will stand and we will fight them. But we will not win. They will take our villages. They will change our ways. They will build their

18

wigwams and their villages where ours now stand. Their tribe will stretch across the land.

"You do not believe my vision, Little Bear. But it is so. It will not happen today. Not perhaps for another generation. But it will come."

Little Bear heard the words of his father. Blue Feather was old and very wise. But Little Bear did not want to believe his father's words, and so he did not.

Little Bear could not think of a different life. He thought of his lovely squaw, Windsong. How proud she and the other Massachuset women were of their pottery skills. They made pottery from clay that they dug from the beaches at low tide. Then they mixed the clay with gravel and sand and shells to give it strength. They wound ropes of clay around a gourd. Then they decorated each pot or bowl by pressing the edge of a scallop shell into the moist clay. When the pot was fired in hot coals, the gourd burned away, and a beautiful round pot remained. Little Bear did not want that, or anything else about his life, to change. He turned his thoughts to all he must do as a brave of the Massachuset.

Now that his new wigwam was finished, Little Bear was ready to hunt. His swift arrows must find food for his family. Their supply was running low. He had spent many sunsets building his new wigwam. Tomorrow he would leave for the hunt.

Since it was still the time of the high sun—the summer—Little Bear would hunt alone. He and the other braves only hunted together at leaf-falling time. Then they would go in search of elk and bear and deer. On such long trips, the men would hide themselves beneath skins near ponds and streams. There they would wait for the animals to come and drink.

But tomorrow, Little Bear would search for small forest animals—woodchucks, raccoons, and porcupines. Little Bear knew the habits of all these animals. He could imitate their calls. And his arrows would find them.

He would also bring home food from the sea. At night, he would paddle his canoe out into the bay. There he would spear the fish that came toward the light of his bark torch. Or he would wait quietly along the mossy banks of a pool. Then his three-pronged spear would plunge swiftly into a silvery trout.

"Oh, there is much to be done," Little Bear thought. And he wanted none of it to change. Before another moon had passed, Windsong and the other women would harvest the corn. This was one of the Great Spirit's finest gifts to his people.

Breaking ground

After four kernels of corn were planted in each small hill, a fish was added for fertilizer.

At harvest, each squaw wore a basket on her back and threw the ears of corn into it.

The women had planted the corn crop with great care, for it would be the last before the snows came. They had broken the ground with wooden spades and piled the earth into small hills. Into each, seeds were planted. A small fish was added to each hill to make the corn grow swiftly. Squash and beans were planted, too. These vegetables were called "the three sisters." The Massachuset felt these crops were maiden spirits who watched over the food supply of the Algonkin.

Little Bear looked past his father's wigwam. "I see the life of this village," he said to Blue Feather. "Life as it was when I was young. It is as it was when you were young. The old ways will never change.

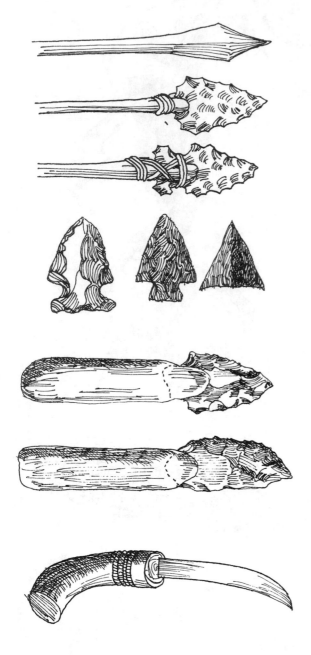

"You see that group of old men gathered around the fire?" Little Bear asked. "They are telling tales to those young boys. They speak of the great deeds of their ancestors. These are the same stories I heard when I was a boy. And when the boys are grown, they will tell the stories to other boys. Just as I will tell them to my son, who is still in his crib."

Little Bear knew that the old men and young boys were not only talking. They worked as the stories were told. They chipped blades and arrowheads from the flint and slate they found on the beach. One man was making a spear tip from an antler horn. Another was fashioning a tomahawk from stone. Still another made a curved Algonkin knife by joining a sharpened beaver's tooth to a sturdy wooden handle. Such work went on moon after moon, in every Algonkin village, for tools were lost in hunting, in working, or in battle. They had to be replaced.

Clothes had to be replaced, too. The women of the village tanned the hides of deer, elk, and other animals to make shirts, leggings, and moccasins. Tanning was a special and ancient art. It took many long hours to rub the

24

hide with a smooth stone until it was dry, soft, and white.

Blue Feather and Little Bear were both proud of the great skills of their people. But they were most proud of the wampum made by the Massachuset and their Wampanoag brothers. This wampum was the finest in the land. It was much prized by the powerful Iroquois, who could not fashion it as well.

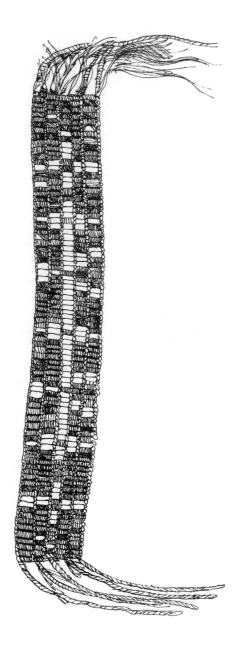

The Algonkin wampum was a thing of beauty and high value. Only the most beautiful shells of the quahog clam and the periwinkle were used to make the wampum. These beads were strung into long belts, sometimes woven as long as a man's body.

Wampum belts were exchanged between nations when a treaty was made. They were carried by messengers for safe travel between tribes. If a messenger carried a belt with a sign of a tomahawk painted on it in red, the message meant war. If a treaty was broken, the belt was unstrung, and the beads were woven into a new belt. Wampum held great power among the red men.

In many villages, it was the custom for one chief to have special knowledge of the wampum. He was called the Keeper of the Wampum. Blue Feather now held that honor. He knew the meanings of the pictures woven into the wampum beads. It was his duty to tell their stories when the belts were shown at ceremonies. When the bark drums beat about the council fires, Blue Feather was called upon to speak the secrets of these precious beads.

Little Bear looked with pleasure at his father's village, so like his own. He smiled at Bright Star, still working on her moccasins. He heard the young men playing the racket game not far from her. It reminded Little Bear of how he had often enjoyed playing this game. He knew that the Great Spirit was made happy by seeing the young men enjoy themselves. But he knew, too, that this sport was good training for the battles that the young warriors must face one day. One team would win. One team would lose. Sometimes tempers would grow hot as they tossed a ball made of a wood knot with their long rackets.

"No!" said Little Bear more loudly than he had intended. "No, my father. The ways of our people will not change. The palefaces will not return. And if they do, they will meet the arrows of our warriors. The children of my children will know and love the old ways, just as you and I have done."

There was no sound from Blue Feather. Little Bear looked down at his father's bowed head. "Do you not hear me, my father?" Little Bear asked. Then he gently put his hand upon Blue Feather's shoulder.

"What is it, Little Bear?" It was Bright Star's voice. "Is something wrong with my grandfather?"

"No, Bright Star, nothing is wrong with your grandfather. He has been troubled, but he is troubled no longer. He has gone to join the spirit of his father."

Bright Star bowed her head to hide the tears. "What troubled him so, Little Bear?" she asked softly.

"His heart was heavy with the vision of the men of palefaces. He believed that the white man's thundersticks would soon be heard in our land. He believed that the white man would build many wigwams here. That the deer and the turkey would be driven from our forests, and that soon we would be driven from them, too. He was filled with pain to think of all this, Bright Star."

"Grandfather was very wise, Little Bear," she said. "Was his vision true? Will the palefaces drive us from our way of life?"

Little Bear stood up, straight and tall. Then he smiled down at Bright Star. "Your grandfather *was* very wise," he said. "But in this, his vision was wrong. Put such thoughts from your mind. Come, Bright Star, we must see that Blue Feather greets the Great Spirit properly. Then you will come to live with my family in our village."

30

Index

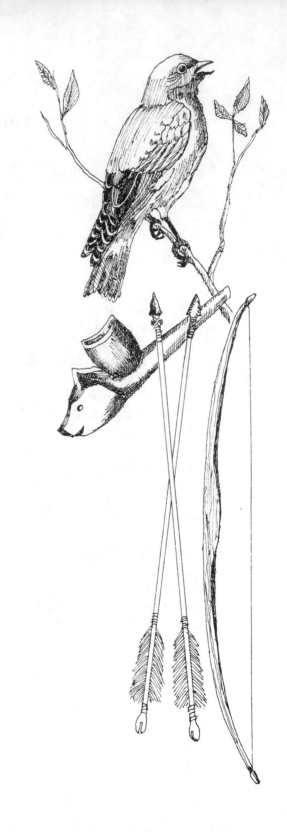